the :01 One
minute
teacher

the One minute teacher

minute teacher

how to teach others to teach themselves

SPENCER JOHNSON, M.D.
CONSTANCE JOHNSON, M.Ed.

HarperCollins*Publishers*

Find out more about Dr Johnson's work by visiting
www.whomovedmycheese.com or by writing to:

SPENCER JOHNSON PARTNERS
251 Riverpark Drive #300,
Provo, UT 84604, USA

Tel: (801) 655 0200; Fax: (801) 655 0202
Email: info@whomovedmycheese.com

HarperCollins*Publishers*
77–85 Fulham Palace Road
Hammersmith, London W6 8JB

www.harpercollins.co.uk

Published in the UK by HarperC
1

Copyright © Spencer Johnson, M.D. 1986

The Authors assert the moral right to be
identified as the authors of this work

ISBN 0 00 720365 9

Set in New Caledonia

Printed and bound in Great Britain by
Clays Ltd, St Ives plc

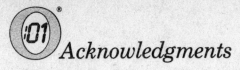Acknowledgments

We would like to give a public praising to the following people:

The administrators, teachers, students, and others who completed questionnaires and gave us the benefit of their experience:

Jerry Evelyn, M.S., Dr. Thomas Gordon, Melody Jendral, M.A., Dan Jendral, Ph.D., Eric Jensen, M.S., Helen Price, Ed.D., Patrick V. Ross, Walter Scranton, M.S., Dorothy Serrao, M.A., Veronica Welch, Ph.D., and Patricia Whelan Lynch.

Kenneth Blanchard, Ph.D., co-author of *The One Minute Manager,* who helped create the format and style of this book.

Pat Golbitz, our editor, who put things in focus.

Jane L. Johnson, J.D., and Hugh Johnson, J.D., for their significant support.

Elmo T. Legg for his belief and support.

Margaret McBride for being our literary agent.

Gerald Nelson, M.D., the originator of *The One Minute Scolding,* for what he taught us about the difference between behavior and worth.

Thomas Payzant, Ed.D., and Gerald Rosander, Ed.D., superintendents of San Diego City and County schools respectively, for their suggestions.

Dr. Carl Rogers for what he taught us about giving each student a sense of dignity and acceptance through self-directed learning.

Kendra Rosander, M.A., for her valued editing.

Ron Zollars and Lesley Kouns for helping to create the manuscript.

And to Joelle Madeline for her caring.

:01 *The Symbol*

The One Minute Teacher's
Symbol—a one-minute readout
from the face of a modern digital
watch—is intended to remind
each of us to take one minute
out, a few times during our day,
to look into the mirror and teach
ourselves what we want to learn.

Dedicated to

Our first teachers: Our Parents

Our Mother, Madeleine Johnson,
for the inspirational teacher
she has always been

and Our Father, J. O. Johnson,
who appreciates self-teaching,
both of whom continually encouraged
their children to pursue education

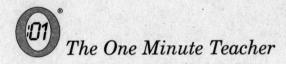 *The One Minute Teacher*

O NCE there was a Young Person who wanted to learn.

He was a student at a local university, who took many interesting courses, read many fine books, and had some very good teachers.

But he was disappointed.

He felt something was lacking. He didn't know what he was looking for, but he knew it was important. He hoped he would find a special teacher who would be able to supply that missing ingredient and teach him what he needed to know.

One evening as The Young Person read the newspaper, an interesting article caught his eye. It was an interview with a successful "One Minute Teacher."

"How could anyone," he wondered, "be a One Minute Teacher?"

After all, he knew, it certainly takes more than a minute of time and thought to be a good teacher.

In the past, he'd often read about the difficulties of schoolteachers. He'd heard of teacher burnout, problems with student apathy, and poor parent participation. And it seemed that many people blamed the problems of society on the schools.

Yet the further he read, the more he began to hope that he had found an answer that would work.

He was intrigued with what The Teacher had to say.

When the interviewer asked her how she really felt, The Teacher admitted, "I once felt that too much was expected of me. I felt rushed and unappreciated. I felt frustrated with students not making faster progress.

"But now that has all changed. I am happier, have more energy, and enjoy watching my students learn more."

"What happened?" the reporter asked in the article.

The One Minute Teacher answered, "I used to be exhausted from my constantly trying to teach my students. Then I taught them to help teach *themselves*."

When she was asked how she learned to do this, The Teacher said it all began when her former principal gave her a copy of a business book entitled *The One Minute Manager*. At the time, the principal had reminded her of a saying she'd heard before and encouraged her to apply it to teaching: "Rather than give a hungry man a fish, it is far better to teach him to fish for himself. Then he will have food of his own for a lifetime."

The Teacher continued, "Teachers prepare students to teach themselves the disciplines of learning. In life, most of what we *must* learn happens *outside* a classroom. I simply show the students three self-teaching techniques. Each takes only a minute. Within a few months, my students were happier. We all had more enthusiasm for what we were accomplishing.

"While the method may not answer all our teaching questions, it is an excellent technique that is extremely helpful and successful for both teachers and students," added The Teacher.

The Young Person wondered what The Teacher and her students knew that he didn't know.

As The Young Person read more of the newspaper article, he was impressed with the teacher's basic principle. It was:

*

*Every One Of Us Is Both
A Student And A Teacher.*

*We Are At Our Best When
We Each Teach Ourselves
What We Need To Learn.*

*

The newspaper interviewer asked, "How can we teach ourselves what we want to learn?"

The Teacher went on to explain that she used an adaptation of the three business "One Minute" principles, first with herself and then with her students: 1. Setting One Minute Goals, 2. Giving One Minute Praisings, 3. Using One Minute Recoveries.

"It wasn't easy in the beginning," she noted, "but with practice it became easier, almost like a habit. First, I used the three simple methods to teach myself. When I did, I became enthusiastic about my life and my teaching. The feeling was infectious and soon my students noticed the difference in me and asked what my 'secrets' were.

"And so I taught them to use the same three principles themselves."

The Young Person completed the article and began to think. His thoughts drifted back to his teachers. He remembered that some of his teachers were well-meaning but the students weren't involved in their learning. Other teachers hammered knowledge into students but robbed them of the joy of learning.

He liked the idea of becoming his own teacher and wanted to know more.

Early the next morning, The Young Person called the One Minute Teacher at her school. She was always pleased to hear from a student who wanted to learn.

The Young Person explained to her that he was looking for answers, answers that he felt she held.

The Young Person mentioned that he would like to learn more about the One Minute principles. "Are they difficult to understand?" he asked.

The Teacher was quick to answer. "No. They are simply a way of *using* methods that you already know work in life, but which you forget to use.

"The key to finding success with the three principles is to *live* them. When we discover that they benefit us personally, we begin to make that wonderful difference in our lives."

"So where do I begin?" asked The Young Person.

The Teacher answered simply, "Begin with yourself."

Then she said, "You can learn more by watching the process in action than from anything I could tell you. I am introducing the three One Minute principles to a group of children next week. Why don't you plan on visiting our classroom?"

T HE Young Person quietly pulled up a chair in the back of The Teacher's room.

"How many of you play soccer?" he heard The Teacher ask. A number of hands went up.

"How many of you have scored a goal?" A few students responded. "Was it fun? How did you feel?"

One student answered, "I felt great!"

"Why did you feel great?" asked The Teacher.

"Because I made it," said the student.

"Exactly," The Teacher said. "A goal is something you shoot for, and when you accomplish it, you feel good.

"What is a different kind of goal?" she asked.

A student guessed, "How about a New Year's resolution?"

"Good," The Teacher responded. "Now, do most of us keep our New Year's resolutions?"

"No," one student answered. "I didn't even keep mine a week. I decided not to fight with my sister again, but it only lasted one day. Then I forgot about it."

"What would help you to remember your goals?" asked The Teacher.

"We could write them down," a student suggested.

"Yes," The Teacher said. "And then you could take a minute now and then to read them and remind yourself."

She wrote on the board in the front of the room:

*

I Take One Minute
A Few Times A Day
To Look At My Goals
And See What I Want
To Learn.

*

"That," she said, "is called One Minute Goal Setting.

"Now each of you use your head and your heart to see what would make you feel good about yourself—what you would like to learn to do. Then write it down as your goal."

The Teacher collected the students' papers and noticed that many students wanted the same things: to be liked by others, to be successful at something and recognized for it, to be happy, and to like themselves.

"Now that you know what you want, let's write your goals in a way that will help you achieve them." The Teacher reached for her One Minute Goal Setting chart. "Notice that we write the six steps as though we are already doing them:

"I take the time to quietly think, with my head and my heart, about what I want to teach myself.

"I write my goals in the first person, present tense. (For example, 'I am listening more in class and now my homework is easier for me.')

"I write my goals briefly, so that I can reread them in only one minute.

"I set a definite time to reach my goal and I state exactly what I want to happen.

"As I read my goals, I imagine how good I *feel* as I am achieving them. The more I *feel* it, the more apt it is to come true.

"I look at my behavior and see if my behavior matches my goal."

Some of the students who wanted to learn took notes. Others paid little attention.

The Teacher said, "Look at your behavior. If your goal is to make new friends and yet every day you eat lunch and spend your time with the same people, is your behavior matching your goal?"

A number of students thought, "This is me." More students began to pay attention.

"Now, who would like to share a One Minute Goal with the class?" asked The Teacher.

One girl, who did not wish to volunteer at the moment, created her private goal in her mind. "I am getting better grades. I am preparing to be accepted by a good college. I feel smart. I feel successful. I like feeling proud of myself."

Another student, responding to The Teacher's request, stood and read, "I finish my homework in time to complete my chores. My father raises my allowance for jobs I've done. I am saving the money I earn for something special. I am having fun making plans."

"Well done," responded The Teacher. "I can almost feel how good you would feel as you do this.

"Now, I'd like you to take out a piece of paper and write another of your One Minute Goals, using the six steps."

When they were finished, she collected the papers.

Some students wanted to hear a One Minute Goal. The Teacher skimmed through the papers and found a good example to read to the class.

"On Friday, I have a B on the math test. I study my math and quiz myself every night. I listen in class and ask questions to be sure that I understand. I feel confident. I feel responsible. I feel proud of myself."

One skeptical student said, "This sounds great. But does it really work?"

"Yes," assured The Teacher. "And you will discover this for yourself when you write your goal clearly and read and 'feel' it often. The more you feel it, the more it works. You will be pleased with the results."

A student said, "You mean I keep myself on target. I find ways to achieve what I am looking for with your One Minute Goals."

"No," The Teacher said and smiled. "You do it with *your* One Minute Goals."

The students smiled. They were pleased. Some of the students saw that The Teacher was showing them how to become their own teacher.

A boy asked, "How does it work?"

The Teacher explained, "You already feel the personal pride of getting a B on the math test on Friday. It is something you feel every time you read your One Minute Goal. It is like riding a bicycle. When you first learned to ride a bicycle, you really had to concentrate on keeping your balance. Now you just ride your bike. It has become a part of you, a natural thing to do. Reading your goal and feeling the achievement becomes a part of you. Then, actually attaining your goal becomes a natural thing for you to do."

A doubtful student whined, "Oh, sure. All I have to do is learn a simple method and suddenly everything is different and better in my life. It's all so easy."

"No," said The Teacher.

"It is not easy. It is indeed simple and does work. But it is not easy to change our mental habits.

"It is not simply a case of learning the principle. *Doing* it is the key. It is only when we *use* One Minute Goals that we begin to learn what we want to teach ourselves. Then we start to feel a change and finally to see a change.

"But only you can do it.

"Most important," the Teacher said, "let yourself have fun doing it. We do whatever we *enjoy* doing most."

In the back of the room, The Young Person scribbled a note to himself. "Learning is more fun when I am able to teach myself."

A student noted, "You said that many of us wrote that our goal was to have more friends or have people like us. How can we do this?"

The Teacher asked, "What kind of kids do you like?"

The student thought a moment and replied, "I guess I like somebody who likes me." He grinned when his classmates laughed.

"Very good," exclaimed The Teacher. "And how do you feel when someone likes you?"

"Popular," yelled a couple of the students.

"I feel good about myself. I really like myself," answered the student.

"Yes, indeed," said The Teacher. "All right, class, who is the first and most important person to be liked by?"

The class was very alert now. "Me!" they answered in unison.

"You are a very bright class," The Teacher smiled. "I see that you all like yourselves a lot." Everyone looked pleased.

"First be a person who likes himself," continued The Teacher, "and other people are more apt to like you too."

One student laughed. "But what if we don't like ourselves?"

"Unfortunately, that happens sometimes," replied The Teacher.

"Then you will want to learn the second principle of teaching yourself—the secret that helps you like yourself, just the way you are."

At the back of the room, The Young Person looked forward to learning the second secret. But first he wrote a summary of how to use the One Minute Goals.

:01 *My One Minute Goal Setting: A Summary*

I teach myself what I want to learn when:

1. I take the time to quietly think about what *I* really want to teach myself. And then I decide what my goals are.

2. I write my goals in the first person, present tense, as though *I am already* achieving my goals. (For example: "I am *enjoying* getting a B in math.")

3. I write down my goals briefly, so I can read them often in only one minute.

4. I am specific when writing my goal. I set a date to achieve my goal. (For example: "I am enjoying a B on this Thursday's English exam.")

5. I use good-feeling words. (For example: I enjoy . . .) Each time I read my goal, I imagine how good I *feel*.

6. I take one minute, several times a day, to stop and look at my goals and to look at my behavior—and then I see if my behavior matches my goals.

Sometime later, The Teacher called The Young Person to tell him she was now ready to introduce the second One Minute method to her class. The next afternoon, he listened as she began.

"You've done such a good job of learning to write your One Minute Goals. Do you want to learn the second way to teach yourself whatever you want to learn?"

Most of the students responded, "Yes."

The Teacher simply said, "One Minute Praisings."

"Is that it?" the surprised students asked.

"Yes," announced The Teacher. "Take one minute to catch yourself doing something right."

"Why do we need to do that?"

"Because," said The Teacher, "telling ourselves what we did well makes us feel good about ourselves. Eric, how do you play on the soccer field when you feel good about yourself?"

"I play better," he answered.

"Sure," said The Teacher, "that is true for all of us.

"When you are feeling good about yourself, and you go to a party, how do you act?"

A girl answered, "I have fun talking to everyone and laughing."

"But," another student complained, "it seems most people only tell us what we do wrong. So how can we feel good about ourselves?"

The Teacher agreed. "Not only do other people tell us what we do wrong, but we do it to ourselves."

She challenged the students. "For example, when was the last time you caught yourself doing something right?

"Why wait," she asked, "for someone else to praise us? When we feel we deserve recognition, why not take a minute and give ourselves a praising. We all want praise.

"Would you like me to show you a way to teach yourself to like yourself?"

The students who wanted to know asked for a practical example.

She thought a moment and said, "I like the way I remember to read my One Minute Goal several times a day. I am helping myself. I feel more positive about my life. I feel more in control of my life. I feel good about my future and my commitment to my goals."

A student asked, "Would you really give yourself a One Minute Praising just for reading your One Minute Goal?"

"Sure, why not? It just may be a good place to begin practicing our One Minute Praisings."

One student asked, "How exactly do I use a One Minute Praising?"

The Teacher responded, "What a good question! You asked for clarification in order to know exactly how you can do it yourself. Keep up the good work."

"Was that a One Minute Praising?" the student asked. "It made me feel good." Then he looked embarrassed.

"Yes," The Teacher said. "Actually, it was more like a ten-second praising." The class laughed.

"To answer your question clearly, I have prepared a chart of the five things you can do to praise yourself.

"I praise myself *immediately*.

"As soon as I have done something right, I tell myself *specifically* what I did right, or approximately right.

"I tell myself how good I *feel* about what I did right. I pause for a few seconds to really *feel* my success.

"I remind myself that I am indeed a good person.

"I encourage myself to continue the same good behavior because I want to feel good again soon—about my behavior and about myself."

The One Minute Teacher suggested, "Perhaps you may want to take a minute now to create your own One Minute Praising. Think of one thing that you are doing right." Then she smiled and said, "I'll give a little extra time for some of you to think of something."

Again the class laughed. They were beginning to enjoy themselves.

After a few minutes, The Teacher asked for volunteers to read aloud their One Minute Praisings.

The Teacher, sensing the students' reluctance, reminded them that we all do something every day that is worthy of praise. She was quick to reassure them that we *deserve* to teach ourselves what we want to learn. And our using the One Minute Praising is a great way to teach ourselves what we want to learn.

Joanne stood and began, "Today I shared my lunch with Sarah because she forgot hers. She really appreciated it."

Joanne sat down and another student commented, "She didn't say how she felt about what she did. And she didn't give herself encouragement to continue the same behavior."

The Teacher looked at the student and said, "Look at what just happened. Let's think about what we do to one another."

She noted, "We often see only what people do wrong."

For a moment the students didn't understand. There was no response. Then one student slowly said, "We criticize people without mentioning what they did right."

The Teacher agreed. She said, "We were so quick to find fault with Joanne's One Minute Praising that we did not notice what Joanne did right.

"Now," The Teacher asked very slowly, "who would like to be next to give us a One Minute Praising and let us comment?"

Everyone laughed. They all knew no one wanted to volunteer to be criticized.

The Teacher said, "We all know what criticism does to us. We silently say, 'No, thank you. I have decided not to participate.' This is what happens when we are harsh on ourselves. We give up and never give ourselves a chance to achieve our goal. What we need to do is catch ourselves doing things right. Every day we do things right, but we fail to recognize our small successes."

Suddenly, it became very clear to one student:

*

*I Can Teach Myself
What I Want To Learn
More Easily*

*By Taking One Minute
To Catch Myself
Doing Something Right.*

*

A student stood and said, "I watch too much TV." The Teacher smiled at how often people caught themselves doing something wrong.

"I read," he continued "that most kids spend eighteen thousand hours watching television by the time they have reached age eighteen. That is more hours than we spend in school. I've made up my mind to watch less television. It's hard because watching TV is such a habit. You said that we don't have to wait for our behavior to be perfect before getting a One Minute Praising. Could you give me an example?"

The Teacher knew the student could do it himself and so she encouraged him to try.

The student began hesitantly, "I have decided to watch less television. I feel good about my decision. Because I feel good, I already think I probably will watch less TV." One student clapped and then others joined in mock applause.

It became obvious to the Young Person that the kids were a little embarrassed by the praisings but they were having fun participating. They enjoyed teaching themselves.

The Teacher said to the young man, "You just did something very important. You didn't wait until you stopped watching television completely before you gave yourself a praising. You caught yourself doing something approximately right— just making a decision to watch less television."

"So," another student noted, "if we can't catch ourselves doing something right, we can still catch ourselves doing something approximately right."

"Exactly," The Teacher said. She suggested, "Let's consider another situation. Say your peers are involved with drugs and at times it is difficult to avoid joining them. Your One Minute Goal is to be absent from drug scenes. Could you give yourself a One Minute Praising anytime you avoid the drug scene?"

The students glanced at each other and nodded yes.

"What could you say to yourself that would help you achieve your goal of avoiding illegal drugs? Think about a One Minute Praising that will give you encouragement to continue doing what you know is right. Now, write the One Minute Praising you deserve."

The Teacher collected the papers, and after glancing through them, she read one of the statements. "I am drug free. I choose to get high in other ways. I feel healthy. I feel safe, knowing that my parents aren't going to find anything they shouldn't in my room. I feel proud of myself. I like myself more. I feel in control of my life. I want to continue the same healthy behavior."

The Teacher described another situation where a student reached his One Minute Goal of earning a B on his history test. She suggested the students think of a One Minute Praising he could give himself.

A student responded, "I achieved a B on my history test. I reached my One Minute Goal. I am proud of my accomplishment. I look forward to showing my paper to my family. I feel responsible. I feel good about what I learned. I feel successful."

"Very nicely done," said The Teacher. "You remembered that the key to winning is not just saying the words. It is important for you to *feel* your success."

The Teacher then described a student who had difficulty with spelling. His One Minute Goal was to achieve a 75 percent on his next spelling test. He earned a 72 percent.

"How could he praise himself?" she asked.

"I've got one," said a student. "I got 72 percent. That is better than I have done before! I feel proud of my progress. I know I can get 75 percent next time. I continue to study spelling and look forward to getting 75 percent or better on my next test. I feel good about myself."

"Excellent," The Teacher said. "Practice giving yourself honest One Minute Praisings. Don't kid yourself. Be honest. That helps you believe in your praisings and that's important. The better you feel about yourself, the more apt you are to learn."

After a few seconds several students answered at once, "We caught ourselves doing something right."

"Great!" The Teacher said. "You have learned the second way to teach yourself what you want to learn."

She said, "Simply catch yourself doing something right."

The Teacher suggested then that the students might want to write down a summary of the five things they could do to praise themselves.

Eagerly the students began their work, following the five steps on the One Minute Praising chart.

:01 *My One Minute Praising: A Summary*

1. I praise myself *immediately*.

2. As soon as I have done something right, I tell myself *specifically* what I did right, or approximately right.

3. I tell myself how good I *feel* about what I did right. I pause for a few seconds to really *feel* my success.

4. I remind myself that I am indeed a good person.

5. I encourage myself to continue the same good behavior because I want to feel good again soon—about my behavior and about myself.

THE following week, The Young Person met The Teacher for an early breakfast. "I must say," he admitted "your students are more involved and interested in learning than most.

"You're lucky," he added.

The Teacher responded, "Other teachers can be just as 'lucky' when they learn to use the One Minute Teaching System.

"It's not really what *I* do," she noted, "but what my students teach *themselves* to do."

Later that morning, The Young Person listened as The Teacher began to explain the third way students could teach themselves.

The Teacher said, "I noticed that during silent reading time yesterday, there was a lot of talking. Some of you complained because you could not concentrate. Do you remember our classroom goal for the month? 'I Cooperate with Others; I Compete with Myself.' Let's look at our behavior. Did our behavior match our goal?"

Several students shouted, "No!"

A student asked, "So what do we do when we see that our behavior doesn't match our goal?"

The Teacher answered, "You can use the One Minute Recovery—the third secret of teaching yourself what you want to learn."

Before the students could raise their hands to ask questions, The Teacher continued, "Usually when we behave unsuitably, most of us either ignore our negative behavior or we become discouraged, even angry, with ourselves. These feelings work against reaching our goal.

"If we want to correct inappropriate behavior, we cannot ignore it. We must first recognize it. As soon as we see our misbehavior, we can use the third principle."

A student asked, "What is a One Minute Recovery?"

The Teacher said, "In football, when someone fumbles the ball, what do they try to do?"

"To recover," the students answered.

"Exactly," The Teacher responded.

"How do we do that?" one boy asked.

Before The Teacher could answer, a girl at the back of the room said, "First, we've got to see we've dropped the ball."

Everyone laughed. The Teacher said, "That's true."

Another student inquired, "So what do we do when we notice we've dropped the ball?"

"Take One Minute to Recover," The Teacher suggested.

"In the first half of the minute, see *what you did* and censor your own behavior. In the second half of the recovery, see *who you are* and praise that."

A usually uninterested student asked, "Which do we do first, get down on our behavior or up on ourselves?"

The Teacher was pleased to see this student's participation. "That is a good question," she noted.

"Look here at the front of the room at this summary chart of the One Minute Recovery. You'll notice that there are a few simple things you can do in a very specific order. You notice it is written in the first person, present tense—as though it is already happening.

"As soon as possible I see when my behavior does not match my goal. I tell myself *specifically* what I did wrong—what is keeping me from teaching myself what I want to learn.

"I pause and am silent for a few seconds.

"I quietly *feel* my 'fumble.' The more uncomfortable I feel the more I want to recover.

"I let the feeling sink in. I do not like it.

"Then I remind myself that my behavior is not good right now, but that *I am good*. And I always have been.

"I redirect my behavior and feel good about myself. I do not defend my behavior, even to myself.

"I recover by choosing new behavior that helps me to learn what I want to know. When I choose new behavior, I feel better. I am happier."

After they saw how a One Minute Recovery works, several students asked for an example.

"Let me give you an analogy," The Teacher responded. "In modern history, one of man's great achievements is landing on the moon.

"In the 1960s, although it had never been done before, President Kennedy said, 'We will land a man on the moon and return him safely by the end of this decade.'"

One student said, "A One Minute Goal."

"Exactly," The Teacher said. "It was clear. The President reminded the nation of our goal."

The Teacher challenged them, "Now let me ask you, when the *Apollo* mission flew to the moon, and landed precisely on target, how often do you think it was right on course?"

One student said, "It was on course all the time. Otherwise it wouldn't have landed on target."

"Wrong," The Teacher said. "That is how a lot of us think successful people live. We think people who get exactly where they wanted to go are somehow always on course.

"In fact," The Teacher informed the class, "the *Apollo* rocket was off course 90 percent of the time. And to make matters worse, a tiny bit off course early in the flight, near Earth, meant missing the moon by millions of miles."

"So how," a student asked, "did they land a man on the moon if they were off course?"

"Because," The Teacher said slowly, "man monitored his rocket's course *continually*. And every time it got even slightly off course, a correction was made *immediately*.

"And that's what successful, happy people do."

She wrote something on the board:

*

*The Best Way To Stay On Course
Is To Look Closely At My Behavior*

*And To Correct Small Errors
As Soon As Possible.*

*

The Teacher said, "Now for some examples from our own lives. Let's make this a cooperative effort. I will show you how to use the One Minute Recovery, but I will need your help. Take out a sheet of paper and write one example of poor behavior, behavior that students your age may want to correct."

The students seemed a little reluctant.

She reminded them that they need not put their names on the paper, nor did they need any long stories.

The One Minute Teacher instructed the class to write, in simple phrases, examples of real problems. She knew they would teach themselves to use the One Minute Recovery better and faster if they used their own examples.

A few minutes later, the papers were collected. Some of the students were eager to hear a One Minute Recovery because it would help them achieve their goal. They were learning.

As The Teacher glanced through the papers, she found a common theme. Before using a few of their suggestions, she pointed out to the class that many of their examples were similar.

She began, "Let's take lying, for example."

The Teacher then gave a clear and complete example of using a One Minute Recovery for lying:

"I just lied. I lied about copying my English homework last night. I think I am lying to my teacher, but I am really lying to myself.

"And it doesn't make me feel very good."

She paused.

"Instead of ignoring it like I usually do, I am letting this bad feeling—one I don't like—really sink in.

"The worse I feel, the more I learn. I don't want to lie.

"My recent behavior is not good, but I am good. I am better than my lie. I deserve to feel better than this.

"Because I am good, I now choose to tell the truth more.

"I feel good about myself, knowing I am more likely to tell the truth the next time.

"I want to feel good again soon."

A student said, "I timed you." Then he laughed and added, "You even did it in under a minute."

She and the class laughed together.

They didn't know anyone would be timing the One Minute Recovery, but it helped The Teacher to make the point.

"A minute," she said, "doesn't have to be exactly sixty seconds when using any of the three One Minute methods—Goals, Praisings, or Recoveries.

"It might take you considerably less than a minute, or it might take a couple of minutes.

"The 'One Minute' is just a small amount of time that you give yourself in order to get a very big reward.

"The point is that we—all of us—can use very little time to a very big advantage."

The Teacher and class agreed that using the One Minute Recovery frequently would lead to more success.

Many of the students, like the *Apollo* mission scientists, now wanted to make their targets. And they knew they had learned a way to do it when they found themselves off course.

"Now I would like you to do two things. First, copy the One Minute Recovery summary chart. Second, pick one goal and think of a behavior that works against you in achieving your goal. Write your One Minute Recovery."

The students turned their attention to the chart.

:01 *My One Minute Recovery: A Summary*

The One Minute Recovery works well for me when:

The first half of the minute:

1. As soon as possible I see when my behavior does not match my goal.

2. I tell myself *specifically* what I did wrong— what is keeping me from teaching myself what I want to learn.

3. I am silent for a few seconds to quietly *feel* my "fumble." The more uncomfortable I feel, the more I want to recover.

The second half of the minute:

4. I remind myself that my behavior is not good right now, but that *I am good.* I redirect my behavior and feel good about myself. I do not defend my behavior, even to myself.

5. I teach myself what I want to learn. I change my behavior and recover.

THE Teacher practiced what she preached. She used One Minute Goals, Praisings, and Recoveries to teach herself what she wanted to learn.

On Saturday morning, she had risen early to have breakfast with her husband. This particular morning, she decided not to join him for their usual jog. Instead, she returned to bed and read the paper.

Next to her she placed a few blank three by five cards. She knew she would be writing down what it was she wanted to learn that week—as soon as she discovered what it was. She asked herself a question, "What do I want to teach myself this week?"

Then she lifted the coffeepot next to her bed, poured herself a fresh cup of coffee, and began leisurely to enjoy the paper.

Later she reached over and wrote something down on one of her cards. It was what she had decided she wanted to learn that week.

As soon as she did, The One Minute Teacher smiled and gave herself a praising in the privacy of her own mind. "I do things more easily now. I have learned simply to ask myself what it is I want to learn. Then I go on enjoying myself until the answer comes to me. I like the fact that I no longer work so hard at figuring things out. I now let the answer come to me. I enjoy this way of creating my goals and I feel more in control of my life. I feel good about myself."

The One Minute Teacher remembered what she had read about Albert Einstein—one of the best people in the world at figuring things out. Even he knew that the important answers never come the hard way. "The answer comes," Einstein said, "while you are eating an apple." Then she smiled. In this case it came while she was reading the paper.

Later in the morning, The Teacher rose, dressed, and went out into the yard. She noticed that the children were still sleeping. Unfortunately, she couldn't help but see the mess in the kitchen.

She thought, "Just seeing that mess and having more work to do makes me tired. If John and I had just taken a few minutes after breakfast to clean up, the kitchen would look better. And I would feel better. I am annoyed with myself."

She paused to let herself briefly feel how tired and annoyed she felt. Then she continued:

"When I clean things up immediately and when I ask for some help, my work gets done more easily and more enjoyably. Next time I will remember to do what works better for me. I deserve better behavior from myself. I like myself."

When she heard the sounds of her children, she went to join them. And later that evening she made a few notes on what she would talk about the next school day.

T HE One Minute Teacher had been asked to present, on this Monday morning, the One Minute teaching method to other teachers in her district.

"Perfect Isn't Possible" proclaimed a banner that caught everyone's attention as they entered the auditorium. They liked that.

The Young Person was glad that The Teacher had invited him and he too looked forward to a productive morning.

The Young Person overheard some of the many teachers in the audience talking among themselves.

They were expressing hope that The Teacher would have an answer for them.

The participants shifted their attention to The Teacher as she began.

"I know you were told I have three methods to share with you. I want to tell you at the outset that I do not pretend to have all the answers. I simply want to discuss what has worked for me and to tell you how I went from discouragement to enthusiasm. In short, the techniques I learned to motivate students."

The Teacher continued, "I have mentioned to many of you that I have experienced both personal and professional growth and success by practicing three simple techniques. One: Setting One Minute Goals. Two: Giving One Minute Praisings. Three: Using One Minute Recoveries."

The Teacher told her peers that before she explained the One Minute principles, she wanted to learn *their own* immediate needs. "This seminar is for *us* today," she said, "not our students." She asked them what they wanted for themselves.

One teacher immediately reacted. "What we need is a better way to get students to listen." Another said, "I feel unappreciated. I work hard and give so much of myself, yet it seems no one notices." Still another teacher added, "I'm just tired, tired of disciplining students who talk back to me." Others said, "What about the bureaucracy and all the red tape we're forced to deal with?" "The public doesn't value our profession."

The Teacher acknowledged their very real concerns because she had once felt that way. Then she redirected their thinking back to where success begins—within ourselves. She knew that while we may not always have the resources to change others, we do have the power to change ourselves.

She turned and wrote a message across the board:

*

The More Often
I Have A Good Attitude

The More Often
I Have A Good Day

*

Although The Teacher was aware that most people in the audience already knew this, she felt most of them forgot to use this truth.

"Our natural tendency," continued The Teacher, "is to look at what is happening around us. But I am suggesting we stop a moment and focus on what is happening *within* us.

"Because we know that our attitude determines our day, let's begin there. Our first One Minute Goal, for *ourselves,* is to have a good day. Let's talk about ways we can eliminate stress from our jobs and have the kind of inner happiness we all would like."

A teacher wondered, "Does this mean that this afternoon we really are here for just *ourselves*?"

Before The Teacher could answer, another teacher commented that when she was happy, she was a more effective teacher.

The Teacher helped her transform this thought into a One Minute Goal. She wrote, "Today, I choose to have a good day because I have a good attitude. I feel new energy. I have a sense of well-being. I teach better. And I feel better."

The Teacher explained, "Even though you don't feel this way right now, this is our goal."

She pointed out that teachers might not be able to change entirely the system they worked in, but they could change their own internal environment. They could reduce the stress in their bodies.

"What do you notice," The Teacher asked as she pointed to the board, "about the way this goal is written?"

Answers came from across the audience. Teachers noticed that it was written in the first person, present tense—as though it were already true. They also saw that it referred to feelings.

The Teacher called their attention to the steps in the One Minute chart.

One teacher called out, "Is it important to follow these exact same steps?"

The Teacher replied, "Generally, yes, because you will find it works better that way."

She continued, "It is very important that we visualize ourselves as already achieving our goal. Let's 'see' ourselves with a good attitude and 'feel' the energy we have. Periodically reread the goal because it will help you keep on target."

Someone in the audience became very realistic.

"What do we do when we catch ourselves with a negative thought?"

The Teacher responded, "I do something very specific. I stop and think a moment. I change my negative statement or action to a positive one. Sometimes that's very difficult. When I don't have an immediate answer, I simply remain quiet and listen to myself until I see a way to change my attitude."

One teacher who knew we are influenced by others spoke. "What if someone else comes in and rains on your parade? Like someone who says 'That'll never work' or 'Why don't you just give up? It's impossible.'"

The Teacher was quick to point out that's why attitude is so important. What we tell ourselves about what we've heard will determine how we react.

"Let's think of a case where we will want to stop and change our behavior."

A volunteer said, "When a student is disrupting class . . ."

Another teacher called the discussion to a friendly halt. "Wait a minute! I thought we were to think about *ourselves*!" The Teacher knew she had a good group.

"We are so used to thinking of ourselves as teachers of our students," The Teacher noted, "we overlook the most important fact—we are first teachers of ourselves. We are here for us today. Let's use an example that will personally help us."

The volunteer gave it another whirl. "Okay. I have been on a diet for three months. I still have not reached my goal. Feeling frustrated and discouraged, I eat. And now I'm gaining instead of losing weight. How can I be positive about this situation?"

The Teacher suggested she begin by looking at her goal. It was positive. It was also attainable. Together they wrote a One Minute Goal. "I weigh 125 pounds. I am losing weight in a healthy way. I look good in my clothes. I exercise for short periods at least three times a week. I eat nutritious foods. I am being good to myself. I feel self-nourished. I feel healthy. I feel confident."

The Teacher suggested, "As you reread your goal often, use your mind and heart. 'See' and 'feel' the success of attaining your goal each time you read it. Look and see if your behavior is matching your goal and then realize how you feel. All this will help you keep on target with your One Minute Goal.

"*Seeing* and *feeling* your success will replace the frustration and discouragement and will allow you to continue toward the achievement of your goal. Your fresh, positive attitude can change your behavior. And you can begin to do it in just a minute."

Another teacher said, "Many of us, myself included, let too much of our schoolwork spill over into our home lives. Can we write a One Minute Goal for this problem?"

Others heartily agreed.

"I'll give it a try," said a gentleman from off to the side. "Every day this week, I am blocking out time for myself and with my family. My personal activities are completely unrelated to school. I compartmentalize my life. I accomplish what needs to be done and I am effective in my work. I feel happier about my life. I feel relaxed. I feel successful."

As he said his One Minute Goal, he knew he was ready to begin to change his life-style because that is what he wanted.

"That *sounds* good," said one of the women standing up. "But when *I* get home *I* cook dinner, take care of my *own* kids and then have to correct papers and plan for at least two hours. There is no time left for *myself!*"

The Teacher knew the truth of what the woman said, but reminded her that we are effective with others only when we are feeling good about ourselves. She suggested writing a One Minute Goal dealing with this problem.

Together they wrote, "Every day I get up fifteen minutes earlier to begin my day by myself, in a way I choose. I look forward to talking with my children, once a week, and discussing with them how we *all* have a responsibility for keeping an orderly, peaceful home. I am also eliminating unnecessary school paperwork by asking myself if I am giving too many written assignments. My children are in bed on time and I am free to enjoy an evening by myself or with others."

The Teacher suggested scheduling a fun time out for yourself each day and you will soon discover how much better you feel about yourself. "Even though it's not true now," The Teacher recognized, "keep rereading and focusing on this goal and watch what happens."

The group began to think about the merits of personal happiness.

The Teacher asked, "Have you thought about the fact that you deserve to be happy? Do you realize that we are each responsible for our own happiness?"

Another teacher suggested, "Let's work with one more example of a One Minute Goal."

A man responded, "I know that I waste a lot of time worrying. I even find myself worrying about things over which I have no control."

"Unfortunately," said The Teacher, "that's true for a lot of us."

He asked The Teacher to suggest a One Minute Goal dealing with the problem. She threw the ball back into his court, encouraging him to participate in writing the goal.

The Teacher was quick to remind him that he didn't have to do it perfectly. "P.I.P," she said, pointing to the banner in front of the room. "Perfect Isn't Possible."

The man began, "I think positively each day. I recognize my worrying only works against me. It solves nothing and uses up my time and energy. I exercise every day to reduce stress and worry. I feel healthy and energetic. I feel free and creative."

The Teacher suggested, "Each time you worry about something, first ask yourself: 'If this happens, what is the worst possible thing that can happen to me?' Most of us have already lived through just about everything. So we generally find we can cope with 'The Worst Possible Thing.' We might even turn the dread of worry into anticipation at meeting the challenges of life."

The other teachers agreed. An older teacher laughed and said, "Have you ever learned a valuable lesson from something good? Or do you learn it from something seemingly bad? I try to look for the good in the events that come my way. It has saved my peace of mind."

Someone asked, "We are feeling good right now. How can we maintain this feeling and stay focused on our goals?"

"One way is to reread your goals often" The Teacher replied. "The other can be found by teaching yourself the second One Minute principle, which we will discuss next week. In the meantime, each of you think about your personal One Minute Goals and begin to use them."

The teachers were motivated and looked forward to learning the second method. They began to think of how their personal goals would begin to change their daily lives in ways they had not anticipated.

SPIRITS were high as the teachers and the Young Person reentered the auditorium. They were feeling more optimistic with their One Minute Goals.

The Teacher drew their attention by asking, "When you feel good, how many of you perform better?"

Smiling expressions on the teachers' faces revealed their answer.

The Teacher sensed an air of anticipation. "Last week," she continued, "someone asked how we stay focused on our goals. The second method, One Minute Praising, helps us keep on target to achieve what it is we want. It supports us by reinforcing the behavior we need in order to achieve our One Minute Goal. And it's a perfect opportunity to instantly feel good about ourselves!"

One of the teachers asked, "How do we do it?"

Pointing to the chart for a One Minute Praising, The Teacher said, "We take a moment to recognize what we are doing right. We tell ourselves what we did right or nearly right. And tell ourselves how we feel about what we did.

"Then we do the hardest thing. We pause in our minds and hearts long enough to *feel* how good we feel about what we are doing.

Several grins in the audience showed The Teacher that some were already having fun with the thought of praising themselves.

One humorous teacher quickly reacted with, "There are lots of wonderful things about me that I have been waiting for someone to notice and praise. Do you mean *I* can be that someone?"

Laughter rose from his peers, for they too could think of deserved compliments that had gone unspoken.

The Young Person jotted a message to himself. "My praise can come from myself."

The Teacher pointed out that some of us are good at giving appropriate praisings to others when we catch them doing something right or nearly right. But we have a blind spot when it comes to ourselves.

One teacher asked, "Shall we praise ourselves for simply making the decision to no longer wait for praise to come from others?"

"Yes," The Teacher said.

Glancing at the chart, the same teacher phrased her idea as a One Minute Praising. "I catch myself doing something right. And I praise myself. I feel good sometimes about what I am doing. And I feel good about myself."

The teachers began to think of things about themselves that were praiseworthy. The Teacher was pleased that so many were beginning to see . . .

*

*I Look At My Goals
And I Look At My Behavior.*

*When I See
That I Am Doing Something
Right*

*I Take A Minute
To Praise My Behavior.*

*

The group was on the right track. One teacher told how he could give himself a praising for starting his vacation fund. For a long time he had thought about taking a vacation but had never really done anything definite about it. Then last week he wrote a One Minute Goal to set aside a certain amount of money each month for a well-deserved and overdue holiday. But he never thought of praising himself for this. Now that he was learning how the One Minute Praisings helped him achieve his goal, he wanted to try one, but was reluctant.

Encouraged by The Teacher, he began, "I am succeeding in making my life more enjoyable. I am doing a good job of putting money away each month for a spring vacation. I feel great every time I think about a change of scenery. Anytime I think about using the money for something else, I see myself on vacation having a great time."

He inspired the audience. Other teachers began to visualize ways to make their own lives more enjoyable. The thought of praising themselves for planning some fun was quite appealing.

Another teacher said she had felt her life was too much of a routine, giving her the feeling of being in a rut. The teacher told of her One Minute Goal to make her life more interesting. She decided to treat herself, at least once a month, to a new and different activity.

Although she had a list of things she liked to do, the teacher explained that *what* she did wasn't so important. It was the fact that a fresh and interesting activity was breaking her routine.

She wanted to personally use the One Minute Praising. She knew it would help her teach herself what she wanted to learn. She began, "I am doing something new and different each month. I am proud that I accept responsibility for my happiness. I've made a wise decision. I feel new energy. I feel alive. I feel good about my life and about my future."

The Teacher said, "One Minute Praisings encourage us to feel good. That's why I always like to begin a school year with lots of them. So I actually 'set myself up.'"

"How?" asked a number of teachers.

The Teacher answered, "Now that you have *first* applied this principle so well to your own personal lives, we can bring it back into our teaching.

"I have a goal," The Teacher continued, "of getting to know my students well at the beginning of each year. I believe it helps me better meet each student's needs. So I begin each school year with basic procedures that have been successful in the past. This way I know I am going to receive a One Minute Praising. It's just a matter of time."

The Teacher continued, "I enjoy learning about my students. During the first week of school, the students write a brief autobiography in class. They write whatever they wish to share about themselves. I ask them to include what they would like to see happen during our class time together."

Someone asked, "Do students like the assignment?"

"Definitely," responded The Teacher. "Students feel a more personal relationship with the teacher. They don't have to wait months for their teacher to know them. It's an opportunity for students to tell you things they want you to know."

Many teachers knew that often students felt more comfortable writing something, rather than telling them.

"When I talk to each student in class, I relate a point I am making to something they are personally interested in. Sooner or later the students tell me they appreciate it.

"In their own way they give me a praising."

The audience liked the idea of setting themselves up for a One Minute Praising. They knew that feeling good about themselves in the classroom would encourage them to do even better.

A comment came from the back of the auditorium. "I've never thought of it before, but the best way to set ourselves up for a well-deserved Praising is to give it to ourselves. It can have a dynamite effect on us."

Someone was anxious to speak. She told of one of their faculty members who could give herself a great One Minute Praising. When morale was low in their school, she was a positive influence. Her upbeat attitude and behavior made a difference to many staff members. A healthy working environment was created in many small ways. A smile, often a few simple words of encouragement, even occasionally flowers from her yard in the faculty room, all helped to create a more pleasant atmosphere. Occasionally she brought in treats in the middle of the week and the teachers found themselves enjoying a social time together after school.

Then she pointed to a woman on the other side of the room and asked, "Judy, have you praised yourself recently?"

The audience laughed. And soon Judy wasn't the only person in the room who realized she needed to use a One Minute Praising for herself more often.

The Teacher pointed out how the positiveness of one person can slowly spread and influence others. By teaching ourselves, we can also help one another.

The teachers' assignment for the week was to take a minute, several times a day, to catch themselves doing something right.

And to give themselves a One Minute Praising.

LATER the teachers listened and learned about the third method.

The five parts of a One Minute Recovery were reviewed, using the same summary chart The Teacher had used with her students.

The Teacher then said, "When doubt and anxiety about achieving a goal begin to trouble me, I remind myself to let go of what isn't working in my life. Whenever I see that I am off course, I help myself get back on track with a One Minute Recovery. I take One Minute to tell myself what I am doing wrong. I tell myself how I feel about it and then I redirect my behavior."

Someone asked, "Why do you use the One Minute Recovery?"

"I use the One Minute Recovery as a fast and easy way to recognize that my negative behavior is not matching my goal. The behavior is keeping me from achieving what I want. And in using the One Minute Recovery, I am careful to separate my behavior from my value as a person. First, I understand that . . .

*

*When I See That My "Bad"
Behavior
Is Preventing Me From Learning
What I Want to Teach Myself*

*I Remind My Self That
I Am Good,
I Am Better Than My Behavior.*

*My Good Self Changes My "Bad"
Behavior
And I Recover.*

*

A teacher asked, "Do you help yourself often with One Minute Recoveries?"

"Whenever I need one," replied The Teacher. "Whenever it will help me achieve my goal. Just this morning I recognized a chance to use the One Minute Recovery."

"What happened?" someone asked.

The Teacher replied, "While reading the morning paper, again I saw negative press about teachers and our educational system. I became angry. My immediate reaction was to place the blame somewhere. I blamed uninterested parents, undisciplined students, and mediocre teachers. Suddenly, I stopped myself. I recognized my negative thinking. I knew it only worked against achieving my goal of personal peace. I then used a One Minute Recovery."

An anxious teacher remarked, "But what you said is true. We are all tired of reading negative press. How can we feel positive about it?"

The teacher commented, "I told myself that solutions don't happen if people are unaware that a problem exists. The press helps keep attention on the issues and concerns that we all have. This was the positive side of the article. I chose to look at it this way."

One teacher noticed on the Recovery summary chart that we redirect our behavior. She asked for an example.

The Teacher said, "When redirecting your behavior, try giving yourself something specific to do. State an action you will take that will bring about the desired change. For example, I want to jog, and I set a schedule for myself. The first week, it goes rather well. Then I notice that most joggers are running a longer distance and faster than I am. Eventually, it bothers me so much I stop running altogether. But I miss it and even feel guilty for stopping. Think of a way I might redirect my action during a One Minute Recovery."

Someone who had been in that position looked at the chart and began, "I have stopped jogging. My behavior is not matching my goal. This makes me feel guilty and critical of myself. I feel tense. I don't like these feelings. [Pause] I am back to my own comfortable schedule of running. I don't need to compete with other runners. I am jogging for myself. I enjoy my own pace and distance. I feel healthy and confident. I feel physically fit. I like myself."

"That was well done," noted The Teacher.

The Young Person saw the One Minute Recovery as programming ourselves for success. He saw once again that the core of the One Minute Teaching System was to help us teach ourselves self-esteem. The more self-esteem we feel, the more easily we learn. We simply reprogram our minds, and our behavior follows. The Young Person had read that our brains weigh less than three pounds and yet are capable of storing more information than all the libraries in the world. With a brain more powerful than a computer, he had great potential for learning.

He jotted a note to himself: "Become my best friend by taking a minute, several times a day, to recover from negative behavior and get back to feeling like my good self."

One of the teachers stood and said, "Some time ago, I read an article about a good sense of humor being positively related to our mental health and problem solving. Remembering that, I've decided to write a One Minute Goal that encourages me to see the humorous side of events in my life. Even though I value humor, I know I am missing opportunities to use it.

"How could I use a One Minute Recovery that would help me achieve my goal?" she asked.

The Teacher said, "We thank you for reminding us how important and how much fun it is to laugh. Today, child-development experts are taking humor seriously. Even hospitals are using laughter as medicine."

The group of teachers then wrote out what they might say to themselves during a One Minute Recovery as soon as they realized they'd lost their sense of humor.

They shared what they'd written, discussed it among themselves, and laughed.

Some of the most embittered and exhausted teachers were beginning to recover.

After the group had a chance to write out several other examples of what they might say to themselves during a One Minute Recovery, The Teacher could feel the energy in the room change.

One teacher at the back, who had always seen the educational system as difficult to change, was appreciating that it was easier to change himself. He said, "And if we change, the system might change."

"This is true," The Teacher said. "I know I want to use a One Minute Recovery in the privacy of my mind when I feel that I am not taking care of myself or enjoying my profession. By that, I don't mean I have to love every minute of every day."

"We're glad to hear that," laughed a few teachers.

"But life is certainly easier if we like our jobs. And it helps to like ourselves. If we do, we do better work.

"I see it is time for us to close. I thank all of you for caring. I know if you *live* the three One Minute principles, you will find greater personal and professional success and happiness, just as I have."

Leaving the auditorium, the teachers felt they had learned something. Perhaps they could begin to teach themselves as well as their students.

The Young Person who had been observing began to believe that by using One Minute Goals, Praisings, and Recoveries, he could indeed teach himself what he wanted to learn.

Then he began to wonder *why* these three One Minute methods seemed to work so well.

THE Young Person soon enjoyed using the One Minute principles. He thought about all that he had learned.

He now realized that Setting One Minute Goals had encouraged him to take direction and responsibility for his own life. And in this fast-paced world, he wanted to be more in control of his life.

His personal and professional goals were positive and realistic, yet challenging. And what he liked most about his One Minute Goal Setting was being able to anticipate success, which stimulated him to achieve. Each time the Young Person reread his goal, and could see and feel it completed, the more he was motivated.

The Young Person remembered The Teacher's explaining that because One Minute Goals are our own, they move us from "I have to do something" to encouraging the thought "I get to do it."

He certainly could see how Setting One Minute Goals worked in some situations, but he wondered about others. The Young Person wanted to learn even more about why the methods worked so well.

Each day, after her classes, The One Minute Teacher enjoyed a thirty-minute peaceful walk through a nearby park. This day The Young Person joined her.

He listened as The Teacher said, "I can tell you that by learning and actually living the principles, we teachers and our students enjoy happier lives. I think we each learn to like ourselves more.

"Our entire learning process begins with Setting One Minute Goals," she continued. "Acting as devices for productive behavior, they remind us of what we want to learn."

The Young Person thought a moment. He remembered reading psychologist Abraham Maslow's *Hierarchy of Needs,* about the importance of meeting our basic needs: the need to achieve and gain recognition and the need to fulfill our own potential.

The Teacher said, "We want to care enough to care about ourselves. One Minute Goals help us see clearly what we really want in life.

"As a comedian once joked, 'What you see is what you get.' It becomes a self-fulfilling prophecy."

As he walked along, The Young Person made a note to himself:

*

*What I See
In My Mind*

*Is What I Get
In My Life.*

*

"Do you recall," asked The Teacher, "the study where students of the same grade were chosen at random and assigned to two different classes? And the teacher was told that group A was above average while group B was below average?"

The Young Person responded, "I know about that study. While the students were in fact comparable, the teacher treated one class as smarter than the other. And at the end of the year, after each class took a general knowledge test, group A scored significantly higher."

"That's right," The Teacher said. "One Minute Goals set our expectations. And when we have high, yet realistic, expectations for ourselves, the result is improved achievement. And those who reach their goals become fulfilled individuals. They become more inquisitive, eager to proceed and learn more. I've seen this many times."

The Teacher told the story of a colleague who was having trouble in his literature class because of the students' limited vocabulary. So, together, the students and teacher wrote a One Minute Goal to increase their vocabulary. They began learning two new words a week. They were doing so well, they chose to increase the number of new words to learn. It was fun for the students when they found themselves explaining to others the meaning of a word. By the end of the term, they had all significantly increased their vocabularies.

"An atmosphere of openness for dialogue between teacher and student helps. Students and teachers can check to see if their goals are supportive of one another," she said.

The Teacher knew that students have their own thoughts, dreams, goals, and convictions. Some are good for them and some are not. With agreed-upon One Minute Goals, the teacher can guide and counsel students in their thinking.

The Teacher also told The Young Person about the teacher who wrote a One Minute Goal to help his students overcome their fear of tests. He had found that some in his class simply failed because of fear or anxiety. The students informed him that they feared the unknown, the unexpected; most of all, they were afraid of failure. The teacher believed that if the students were told exactly what they were expected to know, much of the fear would be removed.

The Young Person said, "Students should be shown exactly what is expected of them. Tests should not try to trick the students. Tests should allow the students to show what they have learned. It's interesting that somewhere along the line, teachers began to think it looked 'bad' if most of their students did well on a test. They were concerned about becoming known as 'Easy Graders.'"

"Exactly," The Teacher said. "But is that true? Does it mean a teacher is an easy grader when most of the students do well? Or does it mean the goal is clearly understood by the students? A test is a lot easier when students clearly know what they are responsible for and what they will be held accountable for."

The Young Person remembered The Teacher's saying that she often returned to her first goal: Having a good attitude. And that other teachers also begin with this One Minute Goal. He asked her why.

The Teacher remarked, "Research shows a direct correlation between a poor attitude and low achievement. Repeatedly, we see students— including ourselves—who do not achieve good results because of poor attitude. Often we do not have a good life because of a bad attitude. And it's the thing we can change the quickest."

The Young Person asked, "Can you think of a time when it was difficult for you to have a positive attitude?"

"Certainly," she responded. "I can think of several. Only last week, I watched a television special called *Parents Are the Primary Educators of Their Children*. It told how the involvement of parents has a direct effect on how students will fare in school. Would you believe 70 percent of my parents did not attend the PTA meeting the night following the TV special? I thought, how can I do a great job with their children when they can't come to a meeting?"

The Young Person understood many teachers felt this way. He also remembered that negative attitudes only breed stress and frustration.

The Teacher continued, "I thought of my One Minute Goal, to have a good attitude. I decided that I could concentrate on the 70 percent not in attendance or I could choose to see the 30 percent of the parents who took the time to arrange their schedules in order to attend the meeting. Whichever way I wanted to view the situation was totally my decision. I asked myself which one would make me feel better."

The Young Person said, "I can see why that would give you more energy." He then asked, "Why is it so important to write down our One Minute Goal?"

The Teacher reminded him that by writing down his One Minute Goal, he could read and review it in only one minute. This would help him "see" what he wanted more frequently and thus make it more apt to happen.

The Teacher told him about the teacher who, shortly after having read her One Minute Goal, began correcting papers. He had been marking the number wrong at the top of the page and suddenly looked at all the minus signs. He then saw that his behavior was not matching his goal of being positive. It was then the teacher changed -20 to $+80$ at the top of the student's paper. He then wrote a positive comment next to the plus grade, knowing that a single word can give encouragement.

The Young Person said, "I overheard someone say that a One Minute Goal might prevent problems before they arise. How can this be?"

The Teacher said, "That's true. A colleague recently told me of a situation in his social studies class. He and his students wrote a One Minute Goal to respect the rights of people who think and act differently from the way they do. This goal began affecting their relationships, outside of class, with fellow students of other ethnic backgrounds, as they checked to see if their behavior matched their goal. The once-familiar derogatory name calling among themselves began to decrease."

The Young Person thought, "When students learn more self-esteem, they may then take the time to understand and appreciate people who are different from them."

He asked, "What do you do with a student who continually does not achieve his One Minute Goal?"

"That's an important question," The Teacher said, "because sometimes that happens. One of two things can be done. It may be necessary to go back to Goal Setting. If the student *can't* reach the goal, we sit down together and rewrite the original goal. If it is a problem of attitude or lack of proper preparation, then we use a One Minute Recovery."

The Young Person thought how well One Minute Goals worked, and in so many varied ways.

He asked, "Do you remember the first time you shared your One Minute Goal with your students?"

"I do," answered The Teacher. "It was when I was first teaching myself to use One Minute Goals. I was preparing my lesson plan and my visiting nephew said, 'I bet your kids would like to see your plan book.' I thought about his comment. For years, teachers have been writing objectives but we made the mistake of assuming the students already knew our objectives, our goals. It works best not to assume anything when it comes to One Minute Goal Setting."

The Young Person commented, "You are saying that clearly stated One Minute Goals help close the gap between students and teachers. Especially the student and teacher in each of *us*."

"Definitely," said The Teacher. "I've seen it work. Before using One Minute Goal Setting, I could ask students what they were responsible for learning, and I would often hear many different answers. Now they know exactly. They now have a better understanding of what we want to accomplish together."

The Young Person remembered hearing that in the beginning the teacher may write the One Minute Goal or the teacher and students may write it together.

Eventually, however, the students write their own goals. They begin with short-term goals and slowly progress and build to long-term goals.

The Young Person told The Teacher of his younger brother, a Boy Scout. The boy treasured his Scout manual because, as he said, "Everything is spelled out." He knew exactly what he had to do to get each badge. And he had lots of badges.

The Teacher said, "I actually close each term with One Minute Goals."

"Close? What do you mean?" asked The Young Person.

"Sometime during our last week of classes, my students give me a report card."

"*They* give *you* a grade?" the astonished Young Person asked.

"Yes," said The Teacher. "My report looks much like my students' cards. Of course, the items to be graded are different. My report card covers everything from class content to class presentation of subject matter. I even have a comment area, in case the students want to add an area I neglected to mention."

Then she laughed and said, "I get some rather amusing comments sometimes." The Young Person admired how she could laugh at herself. He wanted to learn to do the same.

He bet, however, that during the year, she thought about that final report. He asked The Teacher what she did with her report cards.

The Teacher quickly responded, "I learn from them.

"My weak areas," she said, "become my One Minute Goals for the next term. This process helps me to improve and grow in my profession. Remember, I'm not perfect. And it's okay not to be perfect."

"And once I accept that," confirmed The Young Person, "I realize that I am valuable as a person, apart from my accomplishments. I can praise who I am."

Although The Young Person was eager to continue the discussion, The Teacher knew he had enough to think about for now and suggested they meet again later.

KNOWING she was going to meet soon with The Young Person to talk about why One Minute Praisings work, The Teacher took a minute for a praising. She gave it to herself. And it encouraged her to continue the same positive behavior.

"Parents," she thought, "know that the home is an essential element in the development of the character and morals of their children. The home has a profound effect on how children live their lives as adults. So most parents try to live by example, knowing that example is a great teacher." And she, too, tried to set an example to her students. At the time, her class goal was: "Cooperate with Others; Compete with Myself." When The Teacher checked to see if her behavior matched her goal, she knew she deserved a One Minute Praising for cooperating with her fellow teachers. She exchanged ideas, discussed common problems in a positive way, and enjoyed a good working relationship with her peers.

When The Young Person greeted The Teacher, she could tell he was eager to begin their discussion.

"The first thing to remember," said The Teacher, "is that One Minute Praisings are always honest, and deserved. They are a result of good behavior. We all want to be appreciated, not manipulated. I stress this because the success of a praising is based on its sincerity. Be honest and sincere when you are praising others and praising yourself."

The Young Person knew from experience that insincere praise was patronizing. He also knew that all of us, especially kids, recognize insincere praise. It only turns us off and creates understandable distrust.

"People like the One Minute Praising," The Teacher explained, "because it is specific. They know exactly what they did right or nearly right. And they don't have to wait until something is perfect. The young person reminds himself, 'Perfect Isn't Possible.' Each small step toward reaching a goal deserves a One Minute Praising. This keeps us on target and encourages us to continue on."

The Young Person said, "All too many kids suffer from a poor self-concept, created in part by adults. How much does the use of One Minute Praisings help solve this problem?"

The Teacher answered, "I'd say, self-esteem is the greatest result of a One Minute Praising."

The Teacher explained, "We know the primary cause of not learning is having a poor self-image— not a lack of ability. The One Minute Praising allows us to build our self-esteem. It is particularly important for students to praise themselves.

"It's a perfect opportunity for each of us to appreciate and value ourselves and what we've done. We stop a moment to recognize what we do right and nearly right."

The Young Person agreed. He knew he was still learning and his lack of self-esteem could block that learning and make him fearful of progress and change.

The Teacher continued, "When learning is unpleasant, generally the information is not retained. When you want to learn, it should be in a pleasant atmosphere. Unfortunately, not all classes are like that. One Minute Praisings create an atmosphere of success. They allow a student to build his self-esteem. And knowing we are free to make mistakes greatly reduces stress while learning. I tell my students positive things about themselves and their abilities. I feel happy with each success my students experience."

The Young Person remembered The Teacher's saying . . .

*

*The More Often We See
What Is Good About Us*

*The More We See
The Good In Others.*

*

It was obvious to The Young Person that The Teacher enjoyed seeing herself as an "architect," helping to build the adults of tomorrow. She gave her students what they wanted and needed—learning within an atmosphere of success. The students felt better about themselves and their learning improved.

The Young Person said, "We all need praise at one time or another. We share a common need to be cared about as individuals."

"That's very true," responded The Teacher. "And if we want to keep good teachers and develop a renewed, well-deserved respect for the profession, we had better start giving our teachers honest One Minute Praisings."

The Young Person stated, "Students often feel no one cares, no one understands, no one hears them. I'm sure teachers also have felt this way at times. It seems to me that not only the One Minute Praising but all three methods—Goals, Praisings, and Recoveries—show students that we care, care about them as individuals and about their futures."

The Teacher agreed. "I know that honest, consistent One Minute Praisings work. Before I began using them, I spent most of my time catching myself and my students doing something wrong. I made the mistake of simply accepting our successes and neglected to verbally recognize the value of them. Now I accentuate the positive by giving One Minute Praisings."

The Young Person was reminded of the story about a student who was having trouble in math because she lacked self-confidence and had not learned her basic concepts. Her new One Minute Teacher frequently used One Minute Goal Setting and One Minute Praisings with the student. And within the school year, the student was up to grade level. The teacher was reported to have said One Minute Praisings were most beneficial for students who want to learn but lack the confidence.

"Discouragement," The Teacher said, "causes us to lose many students—either theirs or ours. Students may be physically present, but they have given up trying to learn."

"I know that children who grow up without warmth and praise become angry, critical adults," supported The Young Person. "Providing students with acceptance and approval helps create healthy adults."

The Young Person asked if The Teacher believed class praisings worked as well as individual praisings.

"Yes, sometimes," replied The Teacher. "Actually, I am careful of class praisings. You always have some students who think a class praising doesn't count."

"Why is that?" The Young Person asked. "Aren't they part of the class?"

"They believe everyone else is doing well, but they feel they are not," answered The Teacher. "These students believe that class praisings do not include them, so they do not accept them."

"I see One Minute Praisings as strengthening and inspiring independence," The Young Person remarked. "Is that true?"

"We see this all the time with little ones," said The Teacher. "When a kindergartener begins to read, his parents are very excited. They call the relatives to share the great news. The teacher is happy and praises the child. All this encourages the child to continue his small progress. And while the child progresses from single words to sentences, the teacher and parents continue their praisings. But as the child grows older, the praisings are forgotten. It is then that we make the mistake of waiting for something to be perfect before giving a One Minute Praising."

"That basic example illustrates a most important fact," said The Young Person. "In helping myself learn, I need to catch myself doing something right or approximately right, while gradually moving toward my desired behavior or goal."

"You need to remember that achievers aren't born achievers," commented The Teacher. "If I neglect to recognize what I have accomplished, eventually my performance drops or sometimes stops altogether. And neither quality nor quantity is produced."

"This is very true," thought The Young Person.

He said, "I understand a number of students were asked what factors influenced their motivation. And high on the list of responses was being praised or recognized, even when their accomplishment wasn't perfect."

"That's true," The Teacher confirmed.

The Young Person wanted to know, "What other factors did the students mention?"

"Being cared about and respected by their teachers ranked high on their list," The Teacher said. "They also mentioned that being given personal attention and added responsibility influenced their motivation."

The Young Person commented, "So the students were basically seeing positive reinforcement as an effective teacher. If students are to take pride in themselves, they need recognition for their beginning efforts."

He noticed that the advantage of the One Minute Teaching System is that it really helps students recognize *themselves*.

"That's right," said The Teacher. "And being proud of themselves is our ultimate goal. Until the student learns to be proud of himself, he needs to know his teachers and family are proud of him."

The Young Person said, "I can see how One Minute Praisings meet one of our basic human needs. And when we meet our needs, I see both teachers and students winning."

The Teacher agreed. "We are finding that we are more effective in class with the use of supportive One Minute Praisings. A positive atmosphere is created with a One Minute Praising. It takes so little time and yet means so very much."

The Young Person knew that emotional support is certainly necessary for learning. He said, "One Minute Praisings fight discouragement as we learn."

"And," added The Teacher, "they effectively combat emotional abuse, a real part of child abuse. Harsh criticism of children is a form of mental battering."

The Young Person thought, "As we learn not to mentally batter ourselves—to give ourselves One Minute Praisings, we begin to treat others better too.

He looked forward to tomorrow's conversation.

T HE Young Person had been looking forward to another walk in the park with The One Minute Teacher.

He noticed she kept four days a week to walk by herself. And so he treasured his time with the older woman. On his way to meet with her, he thought about the One Minute Recovery. He reflected on the word *discipline,* derived from the Latin word for "teaching."

"It certainly fits," he thought. "The One Minute Recovery clearly teaches me to identify which actions hinder me as I learn."

He knew students needed structured guidance in the form of logical boundaries. The Young Person remembered The Teacher saying that although some may find it difficult to accept, students, including herself, actually receive a sense of security when a concerned adult cares enough to take time for a One Minute Recovery.

As The Young Person approached The Teacher, he recalled the poster he had seen in her classroom:

*

I Know I Am
Not My Behavior.

I Can Change Whatever Behavior
I Feel Is Bad For Me

Because I Always Have
My Good Self
To Draw Upon.

*

"Hello," called The Teacher. "Have you been thinking about the benefits of our One Minute system?"

The Young Person had been lost in thought as he walked along. He was a little embarrassed, but then he said, "I'd like to ask why the One Minute Recovery works so well."

"That's easy," responded The Teacher. "First, we become self-motivated. We get to redirect our own behavior. Second, we become self-disciplined. We immediately recognize when we are not aiming toward our One Minute Goal. And third, regardless of any negative behavior, we have a positive self-image, increasing our self-confidence. I remind myself that my value as a person is separate from my present behavior."

The Young Person began to see that these benefits apply to all three One Minute techniques. He was aware that the more *self*-motivated we are, the greater the possibility of fulfilling our own potential.

The Teacher continued, "With a One Minute Recovery, we simply concentrate on our present behavior, which in turn becomes our future behavior."

The Young Person remarked, "I've learned that unless the recovery occurs as close to the misbehavior as possible, it tends not to be as helpful in influencing my future behavior."

The Teacher smiled and was about to speak when The Young Person caught himself. "I know what you're going to say," he said. "How can I rephrase what I just said to make it positive?"

"Yes," The Teacher said.

The Young Person answered, "I've noticed that when I use the One Minute Recovery as close to my misbehavior as possible; it tends to be more helpful in influencing my future behavior."

"That's right," said The Teacher. "It's much easier for us to do well in the future when we receive clear and immediate feedback on our performance. With our One Minute Recovery, there is no room for doubt. We are aware immediately and know exactly what mistake we made and how we feel about it. We tell ourselves what we can do to change the pattern. And when a teacher can intervene early and deal with the student's behavior, one problem at a time, the student is in a better position to hear the feedback necessary to achieve his One Minute Goal."

The Young Person said, "So a One Minute Recovery works because it is firm, yet fair. It is simply a short, clear, and helpful observation about our own behavior and our concern for ourselves. While it is tough on the behavior, it is gentle on the person."

"That's true," said The Teacher. "Students understand and appreciate that only *behavior* is being disciplined so the *person* can recover.

"Because his value and dignity as a person is not being attacked," The Teacher explained, "the person does not have to defend his behavior. A student merely looks at his inappropriate behavior and realizes that it doesn't match his One Minute Goal. It is not to his personal advantage. It's a perfect opportunity for the student to redirect his behavior."

The Young Person recalled one of the teachers in the auditorium having said that the One Minute Recovery encouraged both him and his students to learn from their mistakes. Students appreciate the One Minute Recovery because it is not a lecture. It takes only a minute or less to use. The teacher liked his recovery because it prevented overreaction or belaboring a point, which we can all do sometimes.

He asked The Teacher if she often used the One Minute Recovery for herself.

"Whenever I need one," she replied. "Whenever it helps me achieve my professional and personal goals."

The Teacher explained how the One Minute Recovery not only helps us attain our One Minute Goal, but helps us see that we alone are responsible for our own lives. "While some students don't immediately understand this, eventually they will," she said. "And they, like us, enjoy assuming responsibility successfully."

"It seems to me that the younger we learn this lesson, the better it will be for us," commented The Young Person.

The Teacher noted, "That is why it is so important to teach the ideas in our schools. And to show students, in a practical way, how to *do* it."

The Young Person wished he'd had such a teacher. He asked if One Minute Recoveries are teaching us that all feelings, even negative ones, should not be hidden or camouflaged.

The Teacher pointed out that not only does the One Minute Recovery show us we are free to make mistakes, but it also shows us we are free to have negative feelings about our mistakes—just not about ourselves.

"Feelings are important," she said, "so it's of importance that we learn to deal with them. We are no less valued as people because we have negative feelings."

The Young Person noted, "We all make mistakes and have setbacks. I'm learning that it is how we handle our mistakes that is paramount."

"Precisely," said The Teacher. "We don't want to run away when things aren't going well for us. In our school, students have become very interested in learning about people who overcame obstacles in their lives and went on to succeed. It's even become a game with some of the students and we encourage their research. A few of my students have a favorite success story about a particular person."

The Young Person was curious and asked who it was.

"The gentleman in question ran for the state legislature and was defeated. He entered the business world and was unsuccessful. As a matter of fact, he spent seventeen years repaying the debts of his partner. His fiancée died. He suffered a nervous breakdown. Reentering politics, he ran for Congress and was defeated. Three years later, he was elected to Congress and two years later he was again defeated. He became a candidate for the vice-presidency and was . . ."

"Defeated," guessed The Young Person.

"Yes," continued The Teacher, "but he eventually became one of the most outstanding presidents of the United States—Abraham Lincoln."

The Young Person was amazed. "It's not only good for students to hear stories of such determination," he said, "but it's an incentive to all of us."

The Teacher smiled and said, "We are, of course, *all* students."

The Young Person smiled and said, "I know, especially when we are teaching ourselves."

The Teacher knew the success stories of others gave both her and the students encouragement.

The Young Person commented, "Sounds as if your students are learning that obstacles are to be mastered, not avoided or evaded."

"It's a good lesson to learn," said The Teacher. "We all have setbacks in our lives. Not always succeeding is a part of life."

The Teacher went on to explain other benefits of the One Minute Recovery. The key to feeling good about ourselves is understanding that we may not always like the way we behave, but we appreciate who we are. And when properly used, the One Minute Recovery avoids those labels, judgments and verdicts that lower our self-esteem—especially the ones we put on ourselves.

"It's interesting," The One Minute Teacher said, "to watch the students become more aware of what they say to one another. As you notice how they change toward their classmates, you can tell that they have improved things with themselves."

The Young Person understood how we begin to accept the consequences of our behavior. He said, "It has been noted that if you want young people to act responsibly toward others, you must give them responsibility for themselves."

He was delighted that he had learned a way to do it for himself.

The Teacher said, "We all know becoming a responsible person doesn't happen overnight. It's much easier for us when we learn responsible behavior in stages. The One Minute Recovery helps us become that responsible person through small steps every day.

"As students begin to accept responsibility for some of their own needs," she added, "they learn that many of the answers can be found within themselves. They begin to understand that it is they who determine the quality of their own lives."

The Young Person had a great deal to think about. He had learned how his and others' success, self-esteem, and personal peace are nourished by the daily use of three simple skills:

Setting One Minute Goals, giving One Minute Praisings, and using One Minute Recoveries.

He pulled a small card from his wallet and read once again the notes he had written to remind himself of the One Minute Teaching System.

A very brief summary of
THE ONE MINUTE TEACHER'S GAME PLAN

How to Teach Others to Teach Themselves

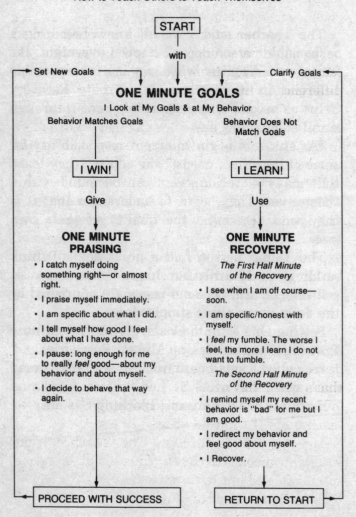

START

with

Set New Goals ← → Clarify Goals

ONE MINUTE GOALS
I Look at My Goals & at My Behavior

Behavior Matches Goals

Behavior Does Not Match Goals

I WIN!

I LEARN!

Give

Use

ONE MINUTE PRAISING

- I catch myself doing something right—or almost right.
- I praise myself immediately.
- I am specific about what I did.
- I tell myself how good I feel about what I have done.
- I pause: long enough for me to really *feel* good—about my behavior and about myself.
- I decide to behave that way again.

ONE MINUTE RECOVERY

The First Half Minute of the Recovery

- I see when I am off course—soon.
- I am specific/honest with myself.
- I *feel* my fumble. The worse I feel, the more I learn I do not want to fumble.

The Second Half Minute of the Recovery

- I remind myself my recent behavior is "bad" for me but I am good.
- I redirect my behavior and feel good about myself.
- I Recover.

PROCEED WITH SUCCESS

RETURN TO START

THE Young Person thanked The Teacher for her time and interest. He was most grateful for learning the One Minute method. It was the commencement of a new life for him.

Many months later as The Young Person looked back, he felt a strong sense of self-direction. He felt good about himself. He had made a wonderful difference in his life.

The Young Person thought about how his learning, growing, and changing had led to a more fulfilling life. And the best part was that he had taught himself.

He was the author of his life.

He recalled how Socrates saw education as a spontaneous process. The Young Person now saw that learning has more to do with living and experiencing, and less to do with a school building, blackboard, and chalk.

His real learning was being able to nurture his own well-being and that of others.

The Young Person now saw teachers in a new light. He thought, "They are planters of ideas and developers of imaginations. People Developers, that's what they are!"

He found what he was looking for—a way to teach himself what he wanted to learn.

And he found, through The Teacher, that special someone to teach him. That someone special turned out to be *himself*.

He thought about his future.

THE One Minute Teacher had become the very best kind of teacher. She was taking time to make her own life happier and more effective.

In turn, she was involving students in making a wonderful difference in their lives. The Teacher was most proud of her students' sense of well-being. She knew something magical begins to happen when we feel good about ourselves. Her students would be better prepared to contribute to a complex and changing society. She successfully met her responsibility of preparing her students for the challenges of tomorrow. The Teacher's name would come to their minds years later as one who had made a positive impact on their lives.

One day, as The Teacher relaxed in the faculty lounge, she overheard the conversation of a discouraged new staff member. The words were familiar. "I spend hours preparing great lessons, but so often I feel that I have wasted my time. Something is missing. So many students just don't seem to want to learn. Why doesn't someone offer a class on 'How to Get Students Excited About Learning'?"

The next day the new staff member came to see The One Minute Teacher.

"Hello," he quietly announced himself. "Are you free to talk? The principal suggested you might help me with some techniques to interest students in learning."

"I'd be happy to talk to you," said The Teacher. "I will only make one request. Simply that you . . .

*

Share It

With Others.

*

:01 Training/Seminars Available

While the parable of The One Minute Teacher has ended, the reality of overworked teachers and underachieving students continues.

Therefore, in order to help teachers, and students, use the ideas in this book, a full training program is being made available, including audiotapes, videotapes, and personal workbooks.

These educational materials help people change realistic problems in the classroom into practical answers for life.

About the Authors

Constance Johnson has many years' teaching experience in public, parochial, and private schools, including two years with the Peace Corps in the Middle East at the University of Bahrain, College of Education, where she taught English as a second language and supervised student teachers. During this time she also worked with the Bahrain Ministry of Education.

In the United States, she has been a guest lecturer on "Parents as Educators." For school accreditations she has served on visiting committees for the Western Association of Schools and Colleges.

Constance Johnson earned her Bachelor of Arts degree from the University of Vermont, and her Master of Education from California State University at Northridge. She is a member of Phi Delta Kappa (UCLA chapter).

As co-author of *The One Minute Teacher,* she adopted the principles of communication discovered by the millions of readers of *The One Minute Manager* and applied them to education, using insights based upon her years of experience with students, teachers, and administrators at all levels in public and private education.

Dr. Spencer Johnson helps people gain better health through better communications.

He has pioneered the field of medical communications for over twenty years, by taking seemingly complex technical subjects and making them more understandable and usable for millions of people.

His work reflects the changing focus in medicine: from physicians to patients to "well beings."

In the mid-1960s, he created *Moments with Medicine,* a series of books to help his fellow physicians learn technical information more quickly.

As a leader in recognizing the role of stress in illness, Dr. Johnson helped reduce many patients' fears of the unknown with his publication in the early 1970s of *Docubooks,* the first series of books clearly describing the risks and rewards of people's tests and operations.

From 1974 to 1979, Spencer Johnson created *ValueTales,* a book series to help children develop a better self-image and grow into healthier adults. His books became the largest-selling new children's book series of the decade.

As co-author of the international best sellers *The One Minute Manager* in 1982 and *The One Minute $ales Person* in 1984, he has shown people a healthier way to work.

Dr. Johnson's education includes a B.A. degree in psychology from the University of Southern California, an M.D. degree from the Royal College of Surgeons in Ireland, and medical clerkships at Harvard Medical School and the Mayo Clinic.

He has served as director of communications for Medtronic, the first manufacturer of cardiac pacemakers, as research physician at the Institute for Interdisciplinary Studies, a medical-social think tank, and as a consultant to the Center for the Study of the Person and the University of California School of Medicine, San Diego.

There are now over ten million copies of Spencer Johnson's books in use in twenty-four languages.